Escape Room

For DFB & ACD
My favourite escape rooms

Escape Room

Bryony Littlefair

SEREN

Seren is the book imprint of
Poetry Wales Press Ltd.
Suite 6, 4 Derwen Road, Bridgend, Wales, CF31 1LH
www.serenbooks.com
facebook.com/SerenBooks
twitter@SerenBooks

ISBN: 978-1-78172-668-6
Ebook: 978-1-78172-669-3

A CIP record for this title is available from the British Library.

The publisher acknowledges the financial assistance of the Books Council of Wales.

Cover image by Philipp Igumnov

Printed in Bembo by Pulsioprint, France

Contents

1

After graduating

In a floury hot room I cranked up all the ovens, cracked fifty eggs
into a perspex bowl, heaved gleaming trays
onto silver stacks. As the market began

its roil and clank, Marie would arrive, crumpling the quiet.
Some days the guy from the deli next door
appeared with a fresh egg sandwich,

hot and greasy, asked me in hard-won English
where's the beauty girl today? And I shrugged and smiled
while she hid in the bathroom

until she was sure he was finally gone. Pains blossomed
in our wrists and hips; stinging burns
peppered our hands. Still delivering sweetness

was not so bad. I took on more shifts.
Life buckles you in. 7pm was my favourite time;
we were so tired we'd cry with laughter and then at 8

we'd get quiet again. And didn't I love
the sugar thermometers? The squeezy bags of icing?
Didn't I hum with the radio, though what the songs

were called, I could not tell you. Isn't time
the finest sieve? Not all of you passes through.

First job

I worked at Boots on Thursday evenings,
stacking shower gels in unnatural colours,
telling blurry-looking women where to find the ibuprofen,
but usually I'd be on the downstairs till,
where a customer came every twenty minutes
grabbing a salad for a late dinner, a stick
of deodorant or baby wipes. They'd meet
my eyes so briefly. Boredom spread
like liquid magnolia soap. Once I picked up
the magazine they kept by the tills –
Health and Beauty, on which
a smiling white woman
played volleyball on the beach.
Suzanne, who was neither unkind
nor stupid, only tired and harassed, said
Don't read that while you're on the till.
There's no one here, I said, looking around,
but I did as she asked and put it away
feeling a twinge of annoyance,
but a strange, building feeling too
not unlike excitement – not because I refused,
but because I was growing an understanding
of what was being asked of me, and I turned
that new knowledge over
in my closed mouth,
like a chocolate coin.

the other kitchen

ben and mark and simon are showing me to my desk ben says here are your penpots there are two and each morning you will move the green pens one by one to the red pot and the red pens one by one to the green. it must be one by one says mark, you mustn't pick them all up in one satisfying clump like a bunch of carrot heads because THEN where would we be. ben laughs a big hearty laugh and claps me on the back so a laugh escapes from my mouth too like he is doing the heimlich manoeuvre. that reminds me i say, will i be doing the first aid at work course? i am looking forward to being calm and skilful and to holding a whole big body in my arms. ben and mark exchange looks. we will let you know they say it might be best if we start with the pens for now and go from there. simon nods sagely before he gets on all fours and begins to meow. ben reminds him that we only meow as a group and that this week's session is on thursday from 3 til 3.30. simon gets up and straightens his tie, he is a little embarrassed i sense so i smile at him encouragingly. now after the pens says ben it is time for the dataset i would like all the data fields ordered by colour i will tell you why later but it's very important and we're so very glad you are here. is there a mug you'd like? we have eeyore mug, sunshine mug and gin'o'clock mug plus some more in the other kitchen. will i be joining in the meowing? i ask mark who i feel less of a connection with but i know it's good to try. we will discuss that at your annual review says mark quite briskly ben will let you know. for now it's best that you have a second go with the pens while we do the meowing. okay i say gamely ben will you tell me what colours you would like the dataset yes he says i will email you don't worry let's just get you all settled in today you haven't even chosen a mug yet! oh it doesn't matter i say anything is fine i say very easy-going and relaxed. no no no says mark, you must choose a mug, we all have our own one you see, it really is important that you choose a mug.

Wilderness situation

He always strolled about and whistled
while we all kept our heads down, working –
have you ever known a girl to stroll about and whistle?

I kept myself still and furious.
Power fizzed inside the desk lamps.

There was a woman with a closed-mouth smile and ambition like a cliff face.
I knew that in a wilderness situation, she'd encourage the group to eat
   me first.

I went to the kitchen to make tea. Milk rested on brown water
   without dissolving.
I returned to my desk and my journal was open.
Each time I closed it, it only stayed closed
as long as I was looking at it.

After I'm gone, I told myself
they'll miss my smudginess and my kindness.
They'll hunch under strip lighting and grow old.

Go on then, you baby, leave. I'll turn off the printers and the burglar alarm.
Take your journal. Haven't you seen that we all have one?

Why did you think it was just you?

The assistant

The assistant is tense and squirrelly. *Oh university* sighs the assistant. *I had this big scribbly heart back then. I was happy as a pig in shit.* Then they look at you accusingly.

If you drop your papers don't worry, the assistant is on the floor passing them up to you before you've even had a chance to bend down. Sometimes they even pick up things that don't belong to you and pass them up with a huff.

The assistant hisses a commentary in your ear: *You know, before I was your assistant, I had big dreams of opening a hardware store* or *Working for you is like chopping off my right arm just so we can shop together for a new one.*

You wake up sweating in the night, frozen in place. The assistant has you pinned. They're behind you in the mirror. They're inside your dream of the Richmond flat with the conservatory and the rabbit and the dog. What if the dog eats the rabbit? What if the rabbit eats the dog?

I feel an absolutely coming on

The clink-clink of it, the hoover of it,
the laid-out table. The tiny nod,
the neat turn down the hallway.
The night-red carpet. You'll be at peace
and I'll have an objective. The absolutely
tingles in my spine. The absolutely turns me
the right way out. I boogie in the hotel lift.
You might finally get some rest
following the stressful diplomatic mission.
Can I call you if I need you? you say.
Absolutely, I reply. My head is a giant lizard head.
But neither of us mention that, and you're too tired to mind.

What a way to make a living!

I'm so bored I want to jump
          into a vat of red paint
stand on a street corner
          like a human postbox

call up the boy I hurt
          eighteen months ago
dredge him up
          like a body from a lake

wear a head torch to the office
          like a caving guide
see if anyone
          looks at me funny

break into my old school's science lab
          dissect one of those
pickled moles, leave it on the table
          with all its parts labelled

get on the floor and bite
          the skirting board
gnaw it and gnaw it
          like that man
who ate the aeroplane
          piece by tiny piece

Lunch hour

Whose pasta is this? he says, holding it up like a scientist with a petri dish, the conchiglie with courgettes gently bathing under yellow cheese, which has melted and reformed like the gravelly ice of a glacier. *Whose pasta is this?* like a dagger in my heart. I'm thinking of the methodical way I'd measured out two tablespoons of light-coloured olive oil, the three pots of herbs I'd taken a pinch of, and the way I'd ground the pepper grinder five times, then set it down, then picked it back up and ground it one more time. *Whose pasta is this?* he asks, holding it up like an ageing newsagent holding a banknote up to the light, or like my mother holding a plaster she's just peeled from my ankle. *Whose pasta is this?* I'd thrown in the last of the pumpkin seeds from the bag at the back of the cupboard, felt a tiny spasm of satisfaction when I chucked away the at-last-empty packet. *Whose pasta? Whose pasta?* The moment stretched out like the moments when a train is boarded, all the commuters kept alive by a single thought: *I am not like these other people.* *Whose pasta is this?* My heart's deflating like the tired balloon it is at the thought of saying *Mine, it's mine.*

Escape room

The employees of Arcantia Investments have just entered the escape room, having been welcomed in by drama student Lucy, who is wearing full early-Medieval regalia and knows how to speak in hushed tones to create the desired atmosphere of fraught but ultimately surmountable predicament.

The theme of the escape room is Robin Hood, the bleak irony of which has not escaped Marketing Assistant Sylvie, who gazes dreamily at a picture of a pheasant, fat with panic in its eye.

Junior Accountant Cameron flings himself to the floor, fists full of puzzle pieces. When put together, the pieces will form the first clue needed to unlock the next room, which is designed to look like Sherwood Forest. He is more earnest than the others, young and energetic, and he says, under his breath, *'come on, we need to work together on this.'*

Sylvie's desk mate Marsha crosses the room and wrestles with the window latch like the doomed best friend in a horror movie. Marsha, unbeknownst to the team, is planning to hand her notice in tomorrow; she had been waiting until after the Christmas party. Her and Sylvie's friendship will not last after she leaves: Marsha will extend a Facebook invite for her 28th birthday party and Sylvie will click 'Maybe attending' and not go.

Cameron, with the help of his boss Alistair, makes progress with the puzzle pieces. He feels his heart pound as he looks at the sand timer in the corner: they may make it out.

[I was going to add in a character here who discovers that the main door to the escape room is, after all, unlocked, and have them all stand in a state of suspended animation. *Should they go on with the game? Or just drop it and walk out the door?*]

But that wouldn't be true. What is true: Lucy has shut the door up tight, and now sits upstairs with her colleague Stephen, watching the group on CCTV. They lean back in their ergonomic chairs like shopping centre security guards in a BBC drama about terrorism, Lucy having loosened her corset. Stephen offers her his bag of crisps, his eyes half closed. Stephen, like Lucy, is studying theatre and wants to join the RSC one day. He makes a cameo at the end of the escape room experience, doing a booming voiceover as the Sheriff of Nottingham, so they have around 40 minutes together until he has to go downstairs. Lucy takes a crisp and looks at Stephen as he yawns and stretches: she thinks she's never seen anyone so beautiful in her life.

Friend

I have a friend, he is an entrepreneur.
He's always barrelling over unannounced,
slamming down two oat lattes, saying *Bryony,*
I've had an idea. Need your input on this one.
I can see his brain trembling. It makes him ill.
I'll just lie down for a second. I watch over
the sofa, pat his twisty brow. Intermittently
he jolts awake, says *what about*
a bear to suck up the CO2? What about
a yoghurt that laughs along with you?
Then he falls back in bed like he's been
decommissioned. Jerks in sleep like a dog
with a nightmare. When he has these moments
of jangling hope, I maintain eye contact
as much as I can, say *Seems like*
you've thought about this one a lot.
He smiles and collapses. Nothing ever progresses.
I don't tell him he's breaking my heart.

The meaning of employable

always changes, used to mean you could whittle or solder
and almost definitely had a dick. Now your genitals can be any shape,
in this part of the world anyhow. And whittling and soldering
don't matter so much. And the meaning of employable
is something else, a bit to do with your handshake, how firm, how dry,
a bit to do with how well you balance sincerity and irony.
But not in a way anyone can define.

                        I want to do a backflip!
I am weak and clumsy, but I could learn. A good backflip is a good backflip.
We know of what we speak. It must be light and springy, legs tight together.
A pleasing arch of the spine. I'll backflip into an interview, quick and light
and maybe they'll be shuffling their papers when I do it – there's four of
them –
so no one would be sure they saw, and wouldn't say anything about it to the
others. All would be feeling funny.
Maybe I had too many coffees today. So the backflip would not be
acknowledged, would not be turned into something else, like
'*oh, I suppose it shows humour?*' drawls one. '*Demonstrates initiative!*'
the mousy one pipes up.

                  No. It will just be a backflip, a perfect, secret backflip,
and I'll be delightful in the interview, but I won't get the job. '*Great on paper.*
But something wasn't quite right,' one will say, and they'll murmur in
   agreement.
Because I created in everyone a private unease, which is not
the meaning of employable, but could well be the meaning of life.

After

Here we are at the broken umbrella museum.
Playing wink murder and refusing to die.

Getting down in the mulch
of the trembling thicket
murmuring to a squirrel
hello, young man.

Some dogs decide not
to retrieve the ball
and instead lie down
in the longest grass.

2

Sunday mornings

The truth is I'm not sure what I did
those mornings they'd leave, my mother
always in a floral capped-sleeve shirt.
I wish I could say I graffitied the newsagent,
or met with a nicotine-fingered boyfriend,
or learned Bertrand Russell by heart. I didn't
do any of those things, nor the homework
I'd invented to excuse my godlessness.
Alone in the hefty silence, I felt loose
and endangered, like an undone shoelace
or an open rucksack. I'd pace from room
to room, hands tucked up my sleeves.
I'd play snatches on the piano, or make
elaborate little snacks – crackers piled
with quartered grapes and shavings of cheese.
I was like a blunt knife, failing to cut
and apportion the hours. I'd spin
on the office chair, or curl up on patches
of carpet, pretending to be dead.
I might have put on a CD, shaken
my hips to Run DMC, a jerky
figure of eight. I might have filmed myself dancing.
I'd be choosing another colour for my nails
when the key would turn in the lock:
my parents, whole and returned,
having sung their hallelujahs
and walked back through the cool light rain.

Swallow

So many times I kneeled, placing the wafer
on my tongue, or a man in white robes

would hold a dry hand to my forehead.
The moment would wobble on its balance beam,

or go over fully on its ankle, and I'd flinch,
not wanting anyone to think I was being

touched by God. Once a tanned youth worker
threw me over his shoulder and ran with me

through the campsite. *Put me down*, I cried,
put me down. How do people

let themselves be carried off?
Another time a market trader

tried to sell me a bracelet, said
Beautiful, yes? as he snapped it round my wrist.

Six years after the last time I went to church
a boy steered me to his balcony to drink a glass of red.

It was 7pm, sunset. I wondered if he'd imagined it – how I
would sip the wine without moving from his gaze

and say *It's beautiful here*. I bought the bracelet.
I never wear it. I'm lonely all the time.

The whole truth and nothing but the truth

is that he made soft noises and I wished he wouldn't
$$\qquad\qquad\qquad\text{that he put on the wrong music}$$
that his desktop background was a stock-image beach
$$\qquad\qquad\qquad\text{sickly with tropical beauty}$$

that I felt pity for him, for this reason
$$\qquad\qquad\qquad\textit{for some people, holidays are all they have}$$
then I felt like a snob   maybe I was the holiday   how about that

—

that he appeared to undergo a transformation above me
which my body had enabled   like I'd died and donated an organ
Here's the thing   sometimes you let yourself   be *conveyed,*
like a suitcase in arrivals   performing your solemn constitutional
hoping to be home again soon

—

that to calm myself   I thought of the different kinds of rock
transformed variously by heat and time   *metamorphic, igneous, sedimentary*

—

that the next day a waitress said   *I feel like I know you from somewhere*
that I felt a sudden whirligig panic   *no*   *I've just got one of those faces*

Self-portrait at high-school graduation ceremony

Look at my fringe peeping cutely from underneath my burgundy cap;
look at my divorced parents who have ended up amicable, gently teasing
with each other. Look at my drama-club mates, rallying around me,
saying 'Go get 'em, prop-girl!', a nickname which is now ironic because
everyone finally knows about my hidden talent: singing. Watch me take to
the stage.

Look at the adoring eyes of the hot jock with a secret love of old records;
who has got into the car with the softness in himself, hit the road and
arrived at me: I am a few pounds overweight but still pretty and also there
is the singing.

Look at my parents standing together, near the constantly stoned but
basically affable guys in my year, who have started to sway as I sing. Look
at the lankiest one, who is hovering next to aggressively dorky science
girl. Watch her take off her glasses.

Look at it all: who is missing? Only Claudia – beautiful, talentless,
calculating Claudia, who we by now understand has an alcoholic mother
and a borderline creepy dad, despite appearing put-together from the
outside: Claudia, rich and sleek like a greyhound.

It's a shame she's not here, because despite her all-purpose viciousness, I
have always been very kind to her, even when she demoted me from the
prom committee for going to a milkshake parlour with her ex, the hot
jock. It would be nice to see her in the crowd, giving a half-smile up at
me, her face scrubbed clean of makeup and pleasantly pink, the face of
someone who has taken up charitable work.

But no: Claudia has packed her monogrammed suitcase and taken the
morning coach out of this town – where to, we never find out – burning
up the road like a fuse.

Tara Miller

doesn't have Facebook. I half think I made her up.
If I mention her to my mother, she sniffs, says
that's the girl who threw your shoe in the toilet.
The one who scribbled on your school report. Her,
who chased me with dandelions; dandelions meant
you wet yourself. But her, too, who threaded daisies
and wrapped them gently around my head, leaning back
to admire the effect. I never went to her house.
A very strange family. Best not. Being friends with Tara
was a desire I could not understand, like wanting
to touch dark, wet paint. Her hair fell all the way
down her back: coarse, wavy, almost black. Once,
when we were changing for PE, Connor and his friend
walked through the classroom: Tara was topless,
in her lilac training bra. I blushed. Tara stared
straight out at them, hands on her hips, unmoved.
I found it interesting, how she wanted me to suffer.
It was a new experience. I spoke of the incidents
as if of a poltergeist, all the time knowing.
Later, I had nicer friends, good blonde girls like me
who put ten pound notes in birthday cards.
Yet when I remember Tara, I remember
her thin white arms around me, her warm,
Wrigley's Juicy Fruit breath on my neck.
I remember her licking her finger,
and very quickly, almost tenderly, reaching
and rubbing a mark from my cheek.

Bait

In this world the topsoil shifts about,
something moving underneath.

Nothing ever emerges, but you need
to be careful, in a non-specific,

all-encompassing way. So let's say
you're going fishing. With your beard

and your bait and your red
plastic flask. You are a sweet and tender man.

Careful! You stopped concentrating
and the soil went crazy, as if with worms,

a thousand of them every square metre.
You have not done

anything wrong. You just want to feel
that tug on the line. You just want

to eat what you've killed.

Gymnastics

Chalk on red raw hands, persistent minor wrist strain –
I couldn't keep up. I was dreamy. My hair fell out its band.
Jo said she'd never seen a girl with stiffer hamstrings.
One dusk I saw her jogging across the car park, keys in hand –
followed, chased almost, by a man in a navy suit.
It wasn't her husband, the soft looking man
I knew from the café. Jo opened her car door.
He grabbed her round the waist, pushed her up
against the car, gripped her throat. I felt lightheaded.
Stars pricked the darkening purple sky. There was no one
else around. I didn't know if she could see me.

Next lesson, as I rose into a headstand, she ran up
and grabbed my ankles, pushed the bones of them together.
Tighter! she murmured. *Try harder.* And I did.

Self-care

Once I was walking out of Superdrug
with £12.50 worth of facemasks

and a man grabbed me by the bicep
and screamed FUCK ME YOU BITCH!

so I strangled him and left him
for dead by the side of the road.

I like making up stories like this.
I like peeling dry skin from my heels

and flicking it jauntily to the floor
knowing I won't hoover 'til the weekend.

Quiet ripping sound

Two things I liked doing as a nine-year-old were eating family-size bars of chocolate and reading about natural disaster in my Dorling Kindersley book *Volcanoes and Earthquakes*.

Breaking off a row of five squares, I would examine the death tolls of Mt St Helens and Krakatoa. *Thirty-six thousand, that's really bad*, I'd mutter to myself as I sucked on the chocolate, pleasure warming my veins.

I was just doing what I liked to do. After all, all those people died a long time ago.

★

I have been in the gallery for 32 minutes. I don't understand any of the art. I tried 'feeling' the art and I didn't feel anything either.

Slender girls in long coats and berets move around the room. Under my own coat, my jumper feels bulky and I am too hot. I've had something in my eye since entering, so perhaps it looks as though I am moved.

I like the sculpture of the mouldy lemon constructed entirely from semi-precious stones.

Registering that I like it, I reward myself with one of the chewy sweets loose in my coat pocket. I slip it into my mouth while the gallery assistant isn't looking. He is sat by the fire extinguisher, wearing a polo-neck which I thought was a neck brace from a distance.

I take off my coat, swing it over my shoulder and the sweets – candy-pink and apple-green, cola and lemon – are flung from my pocket and cascade over the floor, rolling like marbles.

The assistant glides over, helping me to pick them up.

I'm sorry, I say, *this is humiliating.*

★

Today on the sofa
I eat some ice cream – clots
of caramel, dark chocolate fish –
big gloopy spoonfuls. Half the carton.
More. As if the ice cream
is a remote galaxy
some astronomers
just discovered –
but the press release
has not yet been written,
so it's fine that I just eat it.
Swallow it down. Like it never existed.
No one ever needs to know.

3

I love the mighty suburbs

Their starchy economies and long-faced pubs
The contented green of their snooker tables
The pylons trembling in the ripped-jean sky
Chains clanking in industrial estates at the weekend
Dandelions with their clocks blown off, nervous stalks in the wind
The pale thought of a girl in a cellar, wearing a long torn nightie
The newsagent called *No News Is Good News*
The off-license called *Play A Board Game Instead*
The estate agents called *We're Trapped In A Game Of Monopoly And No One Knows It But You*
The estate agents called *We're Trapped In A Game Of Monopoly And Everyone Knows It But You*
The GP called *It's Not Enough Just to Be Alive Anymore, Now We Want To Feel Alive Too*
The funeral parlour called *Fill In The Blanks*
The fancy dress shop called *Party Time*

Heaven doesn't have skirting boards

and I miss them. Hoover bags too.
The entrance is grand, and collapsible.
The air almost frustrating
in its perfect temperature.
Earlier I had a massage so good
that afterwards I could walk through walls.
In the acreage, an abattoir
surrounded by dense forest.

no need for the imperfect things in
a perfect world
domestic spaces become redundant

Say when

I don't really write about, like, war and stuff... I say to my friend, who has just asked me what I write about as he scans the kitchen cupboards for sugar. *It's not that I don't care, obviously I care, it's just that it's not really my arena...* My friend nods. *Mmhmm. Uh-huh.* He is a good listener. He asks me how much milk I'd like in my tea. *Say when. When,* I say, as the milk unfurls in the tea. But he keeps on pouring, as if he hasn't heard. *When!* I say louder, but it's like his body is locked in position, and the milk flows along the table now and plops coldly to the floor. My friend is frozen, jaw tight, eyes darting in panic. *Stop it! Argh! What are you doing?* We wrestle with the bottle. The milk pools and pools.

Juxtapositioning reaction of war with the milk overflowing

Dinner parties

1.

Tonight, instead of food,
our plates are laden
with pieces of paper,
and on all the scraps
are written the ways
we have hurt each other,
betrayed each other,
and let each other down,
ranging from
the inconsequential
to the morally obscene,
including those incidents
both inconsequential
and morally obscene,
in which I am
most interested.
We eat the papers,
each taking our share,
melting them on our tongues
or rolling them
into tiny wet balls.
We eat, and wince,
looking up at each other
from time to time.
And we begin to laugh,
and the laughing loosens
like the evening light.
And then we get started
on the wine.

2.

Love Island *is an exploitative, heteronormative symptom of a racist, neoliberal
and appearance-obsessed society, but I just can't stop watching it!* I say with
a flourish, slightly spilling my glass of wine. I feel a light tap on my
shoulder and there's Jesus behind me with a rueful expression. His white

robes are loose at the waist so I can glimpse his toned abdominals. *And,* he says quietly. *What?* I reply irritably. *You should say 'and', not 'but'.* And *I can't stop watching it,* he says solemnly. He passes me a dishcloth.

3.

There's an extra salt mill
under the table, by my right foot.
Someone must have dropped it.
I can nudge it with my toes.

No one else knows about the salt mill
and I decide to keep it that way

— feeling a little melancholy for it,
as it might not be found now,
until the pub does a deep-clean —
but I don't regret my decision.

We've now been at dinner for
one hour and forty-five minutes.

I don't like these people much.
They make my brain
feel like mown grass.

4.

My friend is always being delivered the wrong personalized gifts. By always I mean it's happened twice. This is a mug for Linda and Mark. There are two photographs on the mug, one grainy one of Linda and Mark holding a big knife ready to cut their wedding cake in 1959, (Linda wearing a high-neck wedding dress with long fluted sleeves; Mark with a droopy but defined moustache), one of them cutting a cake in the present day. And then some red swirly font at the top saying *Happy Diamond Wedding Linda and Mark.*

My friend drinks her tea out of this mug every day. I don't know if Linda and Mark received the mug my friend designed, thereby becoming connected to her by a humming cosmic thread, or if this is the start of a long domino chain of wrong mugs which ends up at an exhausted production line worker tripped up by a file name.

I'm a good person. If I were at Linda and Mark's anniversary party I would make a beeline for the shyest person in the room and engage them in conversation. Make a real point of it. Be with them for a solid 45 minutes. *Feel free to mingle they'd say, shifting from foot to foot. You don't need to be stuck here talking to me all night.* And I'd say *no don't be silly I'm ENJOYING it!* Then there would be a short silence which contained all the world's desperation.

And I would say *you know, I've got this friend and she's always being delivered the wrong personalized gifts.*

5.

The moment arrived late, sweating, a huge ropey bag of junk on its back – balls of string and hardback books, dented tins, maracas, ice-cube trays. *Phew* it exhaled as it shed its bag and took a seat at the table. The moment stretched, looked around at us, took us in. We blushed, looked away. We offered it beans and potatoes from the silver platters on the table. *Thank you.* The moment ate, then paused. *Needs more salt,* said the moment – not unkindly, just as if it were stating a fact.

We are afraid

after Jennifer L. Knox

We are afraid of food poisoning, specifically by undercooked prawns.

We are afraid of burglary: not so much of having things taken from us but of knowing the burglar has been in our house, pacing around and lifting the lids from things; of knowing he could come back again.

We are afraid of other people forgetting our names, as they inevitably do, all the time: you've done it and it doesn't mean anything, does it?

We are afraid of lumpy milk, of the stink, of the effort it will take to dissolve it in the sink.

We are afraid of homeless people, afraid that one day one of them will engage us in a conversation that leads to us giving them all, or most of, our savings – because actually, if you think about it, this would in the long-term lead to a net increase in human flourishing and isn't it therefore the right thing to do? Shouldn't you be walking to the bank, right now?

We are afraid of the takeaway not picking up the phone when we ring to tell them about the prawns (having prepared a little speech with the right balance of compassion and resolve) – of them not picking up and of the phone just ringing and ringing and ringing.

I'm taking applications for my nemesis

and I know that when I find them, things
are really gonna start changing for me.
As I was saying to my friend the other day
(while she peeled a label from an Evian)
having a nemesis is pure and nourishing
like monkey-nuts or red meat. I'll wake up
industrious, buzzing like a lawnmower.
Because wasn't it funny, in that research,
how the rats would rather shock themselves
than go on being fine forever? Anyway,
they'll need to be clever, as clever as me –
cleverer, on some days – and bad, purely bad
so I won't have to make excuses for them
the way I do for my dearest friends.
They'll be ugly maybe, or attractive,
in that hard careless way some people are.
There has to be a very real chance
of them triumphing one day.
We'll arrange to be at the same parties, shows,
and they'll heckle me from the second row
with such creepy regularity
they could almost be mistaken for a fan.

Piper, jester, crook

The piper sings as he's always sung –
with the sort of trembling beauty
that makes the floor fall out of your life.
Your only life – to be clear.

When you come home, the jester has left
all the fruits from your bowl on the table,
arranged into a laughing face. The arrangement
is beautiful, the fruit – of course! – rotten.

The crook leans on his gnarled stick
by the side of the shimmering road.
Will you slow down, and help him?

The need to buy milk

like most of our needs, is not really a need
but something else — a want, or expectation
or something as dirty as habit. Still, I'll buy it,
and I won't duck into that bar in the railway arches
the way I often dream of doing, won't dance
alone in the charged lighting in a manner
both sultry and off-putting. I'll just buy the milk,
go back to my flat and do what I do every Friday night
— watch a hazily-lit, melancholy teen movie
in which people a bit younger than I am
are alternately vicious and kind to each other
in various outdoor settings.

In this poem you are in danger

Not really. Relax. We're in the supermarket.
Look at those eggs dreaming in their gloomy boxes.

A secret: I love it here. Desire moving through the air
like waves of community radio. People tipping things calmly

into their trundling trolleys. You know, in about five minutes,
a stranger will approach you at the till, mistaking

you for her child. She'll hug you, blue eyes watery.
I hope you hug her back. You know that feeling when

you forget to pick something up from the shop, but realise
you could do without it? I hope your whole life

starts to feel like that. I hope your eggs stay whole
while you get them home. I hope you never get what you want.

*Reminds me of ways of Living by
Gemma Seltzer
Suburban aesthetics*

Nostalgialand

wants you back, the sun-warmed seats of its rollercoasters
are waiting for you, the burger you had ten years ago   relatable
which ruined all subsequent burgers for you   moments
is there on a plate, hot still, with ketchup and garlic
and crispy fried onions. Everything is so bright.
You are hungry there in a way you haven't been
for years, your hunger is knife-bright and pure,
a child's hunger, you are crying, everything
is so real. Bunting flutters in the breeze.
You walk into the arcade and ex-lovers
sit up sleepily as you come in
and smile warm as the day you met them,
and some are touching their shirt collars shyly,
looking up at you and down and up again.
But in the strange slow way you realise
during a dream that you're dreaming,
you know you don't have much longer left,
and then someone is saying in a whitewashed dentist's waiting room
no because I've got to pick Kelsey up from school then
or you're looking in your spice cupboard for the marjoram where is it

The bite

I wanted   to bite down   I always do
but today   the wanting was my blood   my nerves
and all their endings   I could no longer   see my life

the bowl and basket of it   blurred   the bite was the island
I had to swim to   the sea reflected the humiliating moon
in its red sky   I hid under the bed   stayed there all night

waited for the wanting   to bite   to subside
pulled   magnetic   to the bite   like the tide
what's on the other side   of the bite   when I open
my mouth   after it   what's inside

my teeth   are itching   my head out of my head
i'm idiotic   done for   like a beach

The Answers

The family man (like the ones
from the thoughtful, middlebrow dramas)
hunches over his laptop
in the upstairs study
face lit blue and impatient, combing
his wife's browsing history,
not in possession
of the answers yet
but about to be –
while his children
gurgle on the landing
and the baby gate
to the stairs
swings open.

—

The ballerina locks up the studio at night, hungry
and exhausted, feet blackberried with bruises,
a dark walk home alone ahead. She might
get a bowl of ramen. One of her toenails
is bleeding. She has failed every one
of her auditions this year
and she cannot call herself unhappy.

—

It's summer and the oligarch's daughter
says to Mary, the housekeeper:
It was peaceful in the woods. I got some thinking done.
Mary looks at her steadily, leant against the sink,
and carries on wringing out the cloth in her hands.

The Twins

is a film starring identical twins
who live in an orphanage
with looming turrets and keyhole windows
and a drive that's three miles long.

It's not a horror or a rom-com
and at no point in the film
do the twins trade identities
or play an elaborate prank on the staff.

Actually they don't talk much.
They don't have the same group of friends.
When they meet in the dining hall or dormitories
they're like acquaintances at a party.

Sometimes on coach trips to the sea
they sit together and catch up about stuff.

The film is really about climate change,
the deleterious effects of sea level rise
in this convivial coastal town.

At the arcade one twin lends the other
a two pound coin for the slot machine.

I realised my life was the subplot

and I was not unhappy about it.
In subplots, after all, angry neighbour
is redeemed, midwife finally falls pregnant,
therapist recovers from kidney cancer, waiter
at the restaurant gets his visa. Quirky aunt stays single,
keeps up her fortnightly visit to the cemetery, laying flowers
on the graves of strangers. I thought I was too far gone, but I'm not.
I'm living in the pool-house. Staying in love. Enjoying my rotation of jackets.

We'll now take questions from the floor

There's a woman opposite me on the tube
with a large plastic acorn on her lap.

A man hobbles over the traffic island
clutching a packet of Space Invaders.

I walk beneath roaring underpasses
to make myself feel holy.

The cashier is showing me
his Deathly Hallows tattoo.

I have never preached to anyone.
I see this as a personal failing.

Working out who to hate
can take a lifetime.

I have this recurrent, blissful dream
of being a synchronised swimmer.

4

Clop clop

People are out and about today
Making their money, making their points

And I'm just putting my hand on your arm
saying *did I tell you about the time I was in pain?*

Then you look down at my hand
and it is a little hoof

last line like a punchline

Room

Would you like to tell me what happened with you this week?

I was in the room again.

Tell me about the room.

No doors. No windows. So more like a box, really.

That must have felt strange.

Yes. I panicked.

Anything in the room?

Nothing. No sofa, no books, no fridge, no television, no bed.

Nothing at all?

Just a poster on the wall.

Do you remember what was on the poster?

It just said 'This is not a metaphor'.

Can you say more about that?

No.

Fruits

Are you cherry-sad? Cherries: late summer
and the swingset, a glacé sadness
that never rots and is never really eaten.

The sadness of pears and apples
grows its tough core in an orchard.
High ceilings and cold floors.
Funeral carts and solemnity.
Gazing at a landscape from a turret.

Vineyard sadness: the sadness
of grapes. The longing to be dissolved
and changed. Riding a motorbike
in a hot and dusty country, barefoot,
arms tight around the torso
of someone you do not love.

Mango sadness: sadness of holidays.
Banana sadness: sadness of the clown.
Lychee sadness: being misunderstood.
Melon sadness: being split in two.

Here is your knife and your bowl.

Some therapists

1. One believed in karma.

2. Another would take a drag on their cigarette and say *fuck it, here's what I think you should do.*

3. Number three took payment in the form of origami animals I had to fold myself.

4. Refused to laugh at my jokes, but sometimes a giggle escaped anyway. I started living for those lapses in composure.

5. Made me speak to them from the next room, so I'd have to shout.

6. Believed in God.

7. Would tell me what they were doing that evening – baking a ginger loaf, going to a wine bar with their cousin.

8. Would say *I'm so sorry for your loss, I'm so sorry for your loss,* over and over – when the last person I loved who died was my Grandad and that was three years ago. It was a peaceful death and he was 91. I'd say all this and they'd just look at me with wet, earnest eyes. *I'm so sorry. I'm so sorry. I can't imagine how much pain you must be in.*

9. Read all my poems tenderly, forensically.

10. Read none. Showed no interest whatsoever.

11. Took payment in the form of poems.

12. Had a pen-pot on the desk when I arrived. Twenty minutes in, swapped it for a candle. Forty minutes in, swapped the candle for a bunch of flowers.

13. Spoke only in nonsensical, reassuring idioms: *Perhaps we could give him the benefit of the snout. Let's call it a play. Hang in bear. You live and burn.*

14. Spoke only in song lyrics, and by the time I realised this we'd already been working together for six months. *We can't return, we can only look behind,* they'd say gently, or *You don't have to try so hard,* and my eyes would well up.

15. Believed 9-11 was an inside job. They never said this, but I could tell.

16. *How can I be happy?* I begged. *That's not the question you really need to ask* they said carefully. *But it is! I swear it is!* I cried, slapping the table.

17. Silently moved their chair around, so they were sitting next to me.

18. Leant forward and said *What is it you're not telling me?*

19. Paid *me.* I keep thinking about going back.

20. Had a rule about eye contact. Look at me, and I'll tell you about it.

Anxiety, mental health and humour all juxtaposed

Sertraline

The summer life was flat cola
I'd wake at ten, a dribble of piss
on my inner thigh, formed somewhere
in the hushed crisis of waking.
Pylons fizzed outside. The weather
was overcast, the ketchup bottle
always almost empty. Happiness
came in jars. It was not serious.
Happiness could be bought
like helium in cans. I feared nothing
only cartoonish things, like walking
through a door and hearing
the lock click shut behind me. At night
I'd dream of the Famous Five,
envy their sexy youth,
their green and bounding storybook lives,
their many and unambiguous enemies.

Lido

Seeing you at the lido was
like walking past a house I used to live in.

Wondering at the blind windows, the grass
just trimmed, the doorstep a brave new red.

Inside things murmur. A drawer sighs shut.
Somebody fishes onion from the plughole,

wet and nauseous between their fingers.
Somebody showers, tilting their face

for a moment to the faucet. Somebody
unsheaths a new record from its case

and music fills the room and it's terrible
and someone is dancing

like they've got no bones, like they don't have
anywhere to be. You looked up just once

then down quickly, then walked on.

Dolphin Cafe

I worried the pastel wrapping paper would make you feel more alone – fat little pink and green owls, beady-eyed on branches. It was all I had in the house. What would have been more appropriate: tissue paper, dark blue.

–

You just got ill. I don't know how. Like it just followed you home one day.

–

You want the beauty of an egg yolk before it spills open. Of the word *lapse*. Of ash poised on the end of a cigarette.

–

I want the beauty of saving you, which is a problem. You can smell it on me.

–

Something in your face is laughing at me, like how all the older girls at all the schools in history are laughing at the younger ones: part affection, part derision, part disgust.

–

When my rabbit had a phantom pregnancy, she ripped out her fur to make a soft, useless nest. The bare pink patches of her skin had a pride to them.

–

You watch glistening bacon rolls be set down on the next table. I watch your face watching the rolls. I speak from behind glass, though there is no glass. Both my hands are left hands. All the spoons are forks.

–

In the dream, when we step out from the time machine, flushed with relief and anticipation, we are still in the present we tried to leave from. I wake up. You are still in the dream.

–

When I walk home later, all the cats' backs are arched and bristling.

I'm always here if you need to talk

Often, I want to do something cinematic for you
like stride in and sweep your dark blue curtains back
saying *Greetings from the land of the living!*
and just before I leave, I want to whisper
something indecipherable and tender in your ear,
something that changes the story. I won't do this,
won't get to. What do I get? Everything else.
I get to have my boyfriend over, to whizz up
late blackberries and lemon in the blender, lick a dab
from my finger, and let there be a beat of silence
before I say *Perfect.*

Men's therapy group

When it came to the end of the session, we all got up very quickly – you could almost hear the collective headrush, like sea hissing inside a conch, as we stood pink-cheeked and dizzy, all aggressively pretending not to have noticed the thing, which was wheezing very quietly and had rolled onto its back.

We were trickling out into the corridor, longing for the furnished quiet of our cars, when someone said *We can't just leave it.* We were all half-annoyed, half-relieved, as when you finally stand up for someone unfortunate being bullied at the back of the bus.

It was something like a soft-bellied mole, the thing. You could see its heartbeat jumping under its tender pink skin. One of us took it home, setting it up with blankets in an old dog basket, and we agreed on mid-week meetups to pass it on to the next volunteer. A calendar was drawn up.

The thing had these shiny, watchful eyes. Except for its chittery breathing, it made no noise. It had eczema, we worked out. We rubbed in the cream with care. It felt good to use our hands again. It wasn't ugly, exactly. It had long eyelashes, and we could see how, when it grew, it might pass for handsome.

The gargoyles sing to Quasimodo

We will sit through the bricklaying present with you,
arranging for a bracing wind at the right moment.

Our suggestions will snuffle up like sweet old dogs.
We will place a green apple in your eyeline.

We won't treat you like a big idea
to be charged along with and then dropped.

We will offer up things that seem enough like the truth
to crack like nuts, roast on skewers and eat.

We will let the birds land on us without fear.
We will take your winded body to the beach.

The path was a river

and I walked it, stigmata maroon on my wrists.
Woman in rags following from a distance.
Beard, etcetera. I thought, *I don't want this.*
Not me. Wish I could scamper up a tree.
Evaporate with the faint sound of bells.
A goatherd. No one looking for me.
No whispering stars. Just udder
after udder. Maybe a staff.   Anyway,
where were we – river. River with quick,
silver fish underfoot. Eating each other. Getting bigger.

Love used to be all I thought about

There is so much to put right. My sleep is terrible.
I wake at five and lie there baking hot.
I haven't made decisions or done the washing up.
At the end I'll be greeted by 1. an unimpressed baby,
2. my first employer, and 3. the smell of burning rubber.
My existence is destroying the planet. But I'm walking
with my dearest friends, who keep me ticking over
like I seem to be most days now. There's a waterfall,
two delicate bridges, some dangling vines stroking
the surface of the river. *It's beautiful,* I say,
like the sweet dumb animal I am.

Climate anxiety + stress
Collective responsibility vs personal enjoyment —
or do the two go hand in hand?

Save in drafts

Every time someone wets themselves, they are a god. Children are gods; when they put pebbles in their mouths, they are especially holy. The time in the pub when my friend told me he had watched virtual-reality porn and said *it was so good, I can never do it again*, that was holy. The manufacturers of virtual-reality porn are not gods. All overambitious works of art are holy. Typos, doodles, Freudian slips: all holy. The silence after you masturbate is holy. Whenever debt is written off the gods are pleased. When someone gives their bonus to charity that's holy; when someone spends their bonus on expensive skincare that's also holy; basically all acts of expenditure are holy, except the purchase of insurance. Every time someone buys insurance, the gods have to have a lie down. People who walk into the road without looking are gods, momentarily. The jokey little poems you write when you're too depressed for anything else are gods, even if they're minor ones *(god of doorways, god of dedication, god of peaceful death)*. Actors are gods in rehearsal but not on the stage. When you put down your drink and fix your gaze to the floor or window and say, *I think I've been sad, I've think I've been really sad* – the gods are there, they are holy, they are shining so bright.

Typo

How am I meant to bear this
– the year a typo in a hyperlink –

wearing a fur jacket to the funeral
like I had to become an animal to endure it.

But yesterday I woke up, cheeks dry for the first time
– we'd slept for eleven hours or more –
and I said, half-dreaming,
                                            I've always thought
lesser-spotted *meant an animal*
has fewer spots but just now I realised
it means less often seen.

Maybe sometimes a strangeness arrives
and lets us free, like loving your partner afresh

when both of you are on separate walks,
and you bump into each other on the high street.

Or a thought occurring to you years after
someone's death: *they didn't do that to be mean,*
they did it because they loved me –

sounding out like a windchime across
an overgrown garden.

                                      It's like the door
being on the latch when the whole time
you thought it was locked. Someone thinks
I can't bear it, and then dies. Typo.
Someone thinks *I can't bear it*, and then does.

Mental health
Suicide?
Regrets and
re-dos,
endurance

71

Escape

And how did you escape, finally?

Did you find the right combination?
Did you jump and hope?

I didn't escape.
I fell asleep.

I dreamt of a bonfire
and woke up in a field of dew.

5

And in the meantime

I try to stay calm   I think about ring-pulls, the pleasures of cans   I google 'deepest hole ever'   I catalogue fruits in terms of their symbolic heft: apple then orange   then plum   then grape   I gargle my feelings like mouthwash of uncertain quality   Oh, my sugary depleted life! My days all chasing their tails!   I wait for something   to rear up   I wait to fill up my body again, quick and silky   as water in a glass   wait to touch my cheeks and find them wet   I am trying to answer the question   Ask it

What am I?

I always have one eye open.
I have two hands, but I cannot scratch myself.
I was trotting before I was born, alive while I was alive, and galloping
when I was dead.
I've left you instructions. If you need me,
I'm in the bath. Not your bath. *The* bath.

The first time I read Frank O'Hara

"And here I am,
the center of all beauty!
writing these poems!
Imagine!" – Frank O'Hara, Autobiographia Literaria

It was 10pm and I marched out of the house –
promised my parents I'd explain later –
and walked very fast, with no destination.

The dark was that emerald,
exciting kind of dark, a gaseous dark, dark
with a lot of light inside it.

All my muscles had opened up,
were springy, easy, I could have run
– I was a panther, a steak knife,

the whole of America, Jupiter and
its seventy-nine moons. Time was hurtling,
I was the ocean, I knew the location

of every trapdoor – and that scent
you catch a few times in your life,
usually in March or April, the smell

of childhood and all your past loves,
that you grasp just a moment,
then it haunts the whole day –

I could smell it, strongly, and knew
I would again. Frank tipped his hat
from across the street – along with

the others, who would come later.
I decided to live in the city one day,
was plotting a pathway out

across the rooftops, and they
would show me where I needed to go.
Who wouldn't want to live their whole life

inside the moment just before the beat drops?

Legend has it

I thought running from love was a way to not die.
I just imagined things would start over, like when
you lose a life in a video game. When you first called my name,
I was afraid. My body steamed up like windows, stuttered
like an engine. I wanted to be on the road again, passing billboards
which only advertise what it might be like to advertise here.
Holly in the back seat saying *everything's a remix nowadays*
Sarah in the front seat saying *there's so much roadkill here*
but really it was the same dead hare we'd driven past
three times. Get in. I'm still afraid but you're with me.
No one's got a watch on and we're here
to see the journey out. Death come get me.
Love come get me. We are alive and moving.

Acknowledgments

Many thanks to the editors of the following publications where these poems first appeared: *New Welsh Reader* ('Men's Therapy Group' and 'Bait'), *Poetry Wales* ('Escape Room'), *Poetry Ireland Review* ('Typo'), *The Interpreter's House* ('Say when'), *The Rialto* ('The whole truth and nothing but the truth'), *Ambit* ('Self-portrait at high school graduation ceremony'), *The Moth* ('Dolphin Café'), *Magma* ('I'm taking applications for my nemesis'), *Under the Radar* ('Gymnastics'), *Clear Poetry* ('Sunday Mornings' & 'Tara Miller').

A project grant for the writing of this book came from Arts Council England when I most needed it. I would also like to send the most heartfelt thanks to other organisations who have supported and enabled me to write over the years: the Rebecca Swift Foundation, The Moth, Mslexia, the Poetry School and Poetry Library, and my UniSlam Post-emerging Cohort pals who helped me make many of these poems better. Thanks also to Kim Moore for her thoughtful editorial report and wonderful mentoring session.

Thank you, thank you, thank you of course to Seren, my editor Rhian Edwards, Zoe Brigley, Sarah, Mick & Simon and the whole team. Thanks to the brilliant Amy Wack who originally encouraged me to send in my manuscript.

Thank you to all the good people who have sent me nice emails, comments, invitations, opportunities, feedback on my poems – all means the world.

Thank you to my creative writing groups at Abbey Community Centre, West Hampstead Women's Centre and Camden Carers. To have you share your writing and time with me is one of the most joyous privileges of my life. General thanks to my colleagues in the Abbey team for bringing a lot of happiness into our corner of the world.

Thank you to all my family and friends. I can't express how lucky I feel to have you.

Thank you to my lovely Grandad, Alan Crawford, who left us in 2020, and to Nadine, who joined us in 2021.

Thank you to Jamie Thunder for seeing me for who I am.

Thank you to everyone who reads or writes poems.